Coming

The Sedro Woolley BANK ROBBERY

Sedro-Woolley Museum, 725 Murdock Street, Sedro-Woolley, WA 98284. (360) 855-2390

Ordering Information
For individual or quantity sales, contact the publisher, Sedro-Woolley Museum, at the address and phone number above or visit www.1914BankRobbery.com.

ISBN 978-0-692-02767-7
First Edition

Front Cover: Deputy Fred Roessel who took a very important part in the capture of the bandits at Ferndale.

Back Cover: Deputies from the U.S. guarding the highways near Cloverdale, B.C. Also a handwritten note from the night of the robbery.

About the Author

‿∿

Rustan Robertson

From an early age, I had a keen interest in the fascinating and rich history of my hometown of Sedro-Woolley, Washington. When I was in the 8th grade, I joined the local Museum Committee and helped to fund and build the Sedro-Woolley Museum, which opened in 1993. During this time, I learned of the "Great Sedro-Woolley Bank Robbery of 1914", and was intrigued by the depth of the story.

In high school, I began researching the bank robbery story in great detail, spending nearly two years and hundreds of hours digging through old newspapers and public records from Skagit County to Canada, following leads and clues, and cross-referencing details. I had the good fortune to be able to interview both the daughter of head cashier John Guddall, and the son of Skagit County Sheriff Ed Wells. I found the graves of young Melvin Wilson and Canadian officer Clifford Adams, as well as the unmarked graves of two of the four dead bank robbers. And I was thrilled to come to the realization that not only was this event well documented in writing, but a series of over 100 glass lantern slides had been produced with spectacular shots of the aftermath of the robbery, which you will see in the following pages. *Note that the photo captions follow the language (and spelling) of the original script that accompanied the glass lantern slides.*

After wrapping up my research as part of my high school Senior Project in 1996, my materials gathered dust until 2014 when I decided to partner with the Sedro-Woolley Museum to produce this book in commemoration of the 100th anniversary of the robbery. The Museum had teamed up with the Washington State Archives office to scan the original glass lantern slides to digital formats, so this was a great opportunity to combine the photos with the story to produce a complete account of the events that took place in October of 1914.

If there is one lesson from this story that stands out from others for me, it is that history is happening around us every single day, and it's there for us to record and remember - today. The community members in 1914 could easily have cleaned up and gone on with their lives. Instead, somebody had the foresight to produce images to record this series of events, and those historical assets have lived on. I am forever grateful to those individuals, and I hope you enjoy this snapshot in history.

Acknowledgements

First and foremost, I would like to thank the Sedro-Woolley Museum and its Board of Directors for their commitment to this project, including financial backing, time, and the use of the photos from the original set of glass lantern slides. Additionally, I would like to thank Carolyn Freeman and Belle Canaday for their time and efforts in planning for this project, in addition to their longtime friendship, and dedication to the Museum.

The Washington State Archives for use of their technology in scanning the original glass lantern slides and resulting digital files.

Roger Peterson for research of the downtown Sedro-Woolley businesses, and for the map showing locations of businesses in October of 1914.

Ed and Donna Marlow, and John Ruthford for the use of the photo collection during my original research in 1996.

The Lemley and Wells families for interviews during my initial research.

Kathy Reim for encouragement and guidance as my high school English teacher while I was compiling research and piecing the story together.

Bellingham Public Library and Washington State Archives in Bellingham, along with Whatcom County for use of their archives of newspapers and documents.

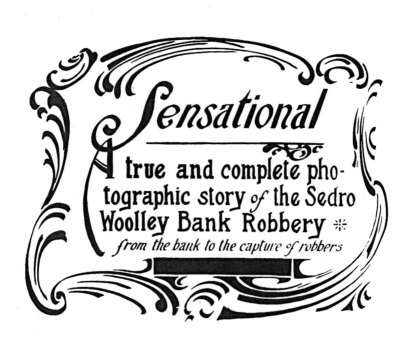

Sensational

A true and complete photographic story of the Sedro Woolley Bank Robbery ❋

from the bank to the capture of robbers

1
Setting the Stage

I n the early 20th century, Sedro-Woolley, Washington was an average American community in many respects. The small town, which emerged from the joining of two communities in 1898, was basically quiet and nondescript. That friendly silence was broken, though on the night of Saturday, October 17, 1914, when five armed bandits held up the First National Bank on Sedro-Woolley's main street, with an ensuing shootout that resulted in one death, two injuries, the loss of nearly $12,000, and a downtown perforated with bullets. The following bandit hunt led posses into Canada and the northernmost edges of Washington State before the bandits were finally killed.

View of the main street of Sedro-Woolley looking north.

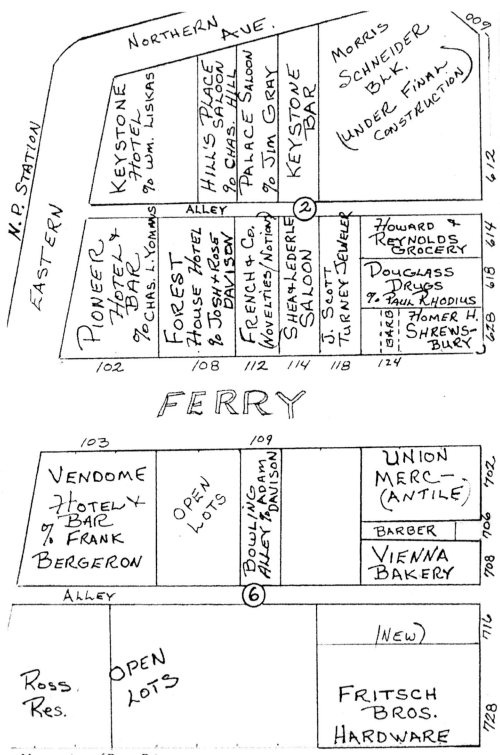

NORTHERN AVE.

009

N. P. STATION

EASTERN

KEYSTONE HOTEL ℅ WM. LISKAS

HILL'S PLACE SALOON ℅ CHAS. HILL

PALACE SALOON ℅ JIM GRAY

KEYSTONE BAR

MORRIS SCHNEIDER BLK. (UNDER FINAL CONSTRUCTION)

612

ALLEY

②

PIONEER HOTEL + BAR ℅ CHAS. L. YOMANS

FOREST HOUSE HOTEL ℅ JOSH + ROSS DAVISON

FRENCH + CO. (NOVELTIES/NOTIONS)

SHEA + LEDERLE SALOON

J. SCOTT TURNEY JEWELER

HOWARD + REYNOLDS GROCERY

614

DOUGLASS DRUGS ℅ PAUL RHODIUS

618

BARB

HOMER H. SHREWS-BURY

678

102   108   112   114   118   124

FERRY

103   109

VENDOME HOTEL + BAR ℅ FRANK BERGERON

OPEN LOTS

BOWLING ALLEY ℅ ADAM DAVISON

UNION MERC— (ANTILE)

702

BARBER   706

VIENNA BAKERY   708

ALLEY

⑥

ROSS. RES.

OPEN LOTS

716

(NEW)

FRITSCH BROS. HARDWARE

728

Map courtesy of Roger Peterson

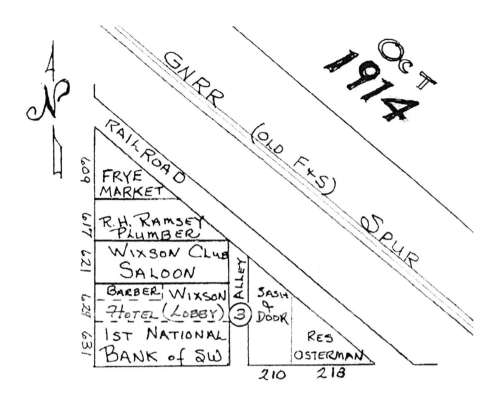

Oct 1914

N

GNRR (old F+S) SPUR

609 FRYE MARKET

617 R.H. RAMSEY PLUMBER

621 WIXSON CLUB SALOON

629 BARBER WIXSON HOTEL (LOBBY)

631 1ST NATIONAL BANK of SW

RAILROAD

ALLEY

③ SASH & DOOR

RES OSTERMAN

210   218

METCALF

207 211

701 J.F. MOTT DRUGS

705 707 CODDINGTON'S DRY GOODS

707 SWASTIKA CAFE

709 CHAS. H. NYE CONFECTIONARY

TAILOR LAW

OPEN LOTS

JIM GRAY RES

⑤ ALLEY

711 H. CONDY JEWELRY

713 GEO. R. CLARK HABERDASHERY

715 ADOLPH BAUER SHOES

729 STAR GROCERY

DREAM THEATRE

EUSTIN REND RES × BICYCLE SHOP

216   220

The action began in Sedro-Woolley over a week before the actual robbery. Several suspicious men had been seen loitering around Sedro-Woolley's pool rooms, arriving in town in the afternoon and leaving just after dark. On one occasion, they purchased white shirts and collars at one of Sedro-Woolley's clothiers, which they would later be seen wearing on the night of the robbery.

The evening of Saturday, October 10, 1914, John Guddall, the manager of the First National Bank, left after dark for his daily trip to the post office. While he was gone, a suspicious man went into the bank to change a $5 gold piece, and supposedly asked the cashier if he was alone. The spooked cashier replied that Guddall would be back anytime, and as luck would have it, he walked in just as the man was leaving. Guddall immediately closed the iron gates at the main entrance and exited through

The bank situated on the northeast corner and the building containing also the Wixson Hotel and a pool-room.

the back door. He proceeded just to the south to the Dream Theatre on Woodworth Street, where he phoned the nearby Bingham Bank staff to warn them of the suspicious character. Word came just in time, and the bank personnel were able to secure their establishment just before the suspect arrived. Frustrated, the man and his presumed accomplices left the scene.

Guddall informed the police of the encounter, and they began to make preparations for extra surveillance and protection at the two banks in case the men attempted a robbery in the near future. A surplus of ammunition was placed throughout the bank in reach of the employees, and Mr. Guddall placed a large .38 revolver under his teller window. He advised the young lady who worked in his office that she was not to report to work the following week.

A street scene taken at night, showing the situation of the lights at the time of the robbery. Later the lights of the bank being put out left the robbers in the dark and the officers and citizens of Sedro-Woolley in the light, giving all possible advantage to the robbers.

2

The Robbery

The week of October 12th began without incident. However, as the week went on, there had been sightings of some more suspicious folks, which raised concern of a possible threat again on Saturday. After discussing the possibility of another robbery attempt, local law enforcement decided to make serious preparations for such a threat. Marshal Charles Villeneuve was assigned to coordinate an ad hoc posse, and on Saturday, October 17th, 1914, made final arrangements to prepare, should a robbery attempt take place.

Marshal Villeneuve sought the assistance of Deputy Marshal Jasper Holman, Frank Hoehn, local bartender Fred Carlin, and Rolly Beebe, and the men gathered in town. Following an uneventful morning and afternoon, Guddall returned to the bank in the early evening just after supper. Villeneuve and Holman were there, and the three men conversed. Hoehn and Carlin were also nearby, and after Guddall entered the bank, Holman assured Hoehn that other officers were stationed nearby as well. Following the conversation, Villeneuve was called across the street near Mott's Drug Store to address a disturbance. He called Holman to join him by the Union Mercantile Building, and the two men continued west on Ferry Street to the Vendome Hotel, a block away. A woman who appeared to be under the influence of alcohol was causing trouble, and the two men attempted to resolve the problem. Meanwhile, Beebe remained at his post a block south of the First National Bank near the Bingham Bank.

Just after Villeneuve and Holman arrived at the hotel, the bandits who had apparently been hiding in the area, crossed the street from near the Shrewsbury Hardware store (just across from the bank) and stationed themselves around the bank. Two stood outside the entrance. A third was behind a lamppost near the bank, a fourth remained across the street, and a fifth – after seeing that there was a large group of hunters

Officer Jasper Holman of Sedro-Woolley.

Officer Villeneuve. This officer being stationed at the bank was driven across the street, hiding directly behind Mr. Mott's Drug Store, he emptied his rifle and revolver at the bandits. While returning to the police station for more ammunition the robbery was completed.

eating supper at the Wixson restaurant who might cause trouble for them – stationed himself there.

Unsuspecting bank customer, local grocery store proprietor F.A. Hegg, went into the bank to make his nightly deposit. Just then, two of the bandits ran inside the bank shouting, "Hands up!" Hegg ducked under the arm of one of the men and quickly exited the building. Guddall raised both hands, but in his right was his .38 revolver. He shot point blank at the men, missing both. He would later explain that he was trying to attract the attention of the police rather than trying to kill the robbers. Two other bandits, knowing their two partners would soon need help, walked east on Ferry Street to the rear of the bank and prepared to enter.

The shootout continued for some time between Guddall and the two robbers in the bank lobby, as bank assistant J. Marsden and bookkeeper Frank Lebold crouched safely behind their desks. The robbers also

Chief of police Beebe. Officer Beebe being armed with a .38 Automatic Rifle was stationed at the other bank. When the firing started, he attempted to advance up the street. Finding that impossible, he went into an alley by the Vienna bakery, emptying his rifle, also his revolver at the bandits.

assumed positions on the floor in front of the counter and proceeded to shoot through the thick wood, trying in vain to wound Guddall or scare him into giving up.

The bandits behind the bank took the plethora of gunshots as a signal to join the action, and proceeded to shoot out plate glass windows of nearby businesses in an attempt to scare citizens and keep them from interfering with the heist.

Hoehn and Carlin, who were standing nearby, quickly realized they were in danger. "We had better get out of here," Carlin yelled. They began running towards the Hoehn barn just a block east of the bank, but had only gotten about 15 yards when Carlin was shot in his left leg between the knee and thigh. Hoehn grabbed Carlin by the arm and pulled him out of danger. "As I helped Carlin away, I expected to be shot down at every step," Hoehn would later say.

This is Mr. Carlin, who was wounded in the leg while crossing the street, by a bullet from one of the bandits. After becoming a deputy, he was very active in the final capture of the robbers.

Mr. Guddall, the cashier of the bank, was brave and plucky and fought until he was cornered, but finally had to open the vaults.

Mr. Frank Lebold, the Book-keeper of the F.N. Bank, who was sitting on a stool at his work, with a gun at easy reach when the robbery occurred, but was unable to use it.

Mr. J. Marsden, the assistant cashier showing a bullet hole in his coat through which the bullet had passed.

Showing the method the robbers used in entering and shooting up the bank. They ducked down beneath the counter, where bandits shot through with the intent to cripple Cashier.

Villeneuve and Holman, who were by this time on their way back from the ruckus at the Vendome Hotel and were nearing the bank, quickly joined the action. Frank O'Conner also joined them after having been given a gun by Villeneuve. Villeneuve emptied his own automatic towards the bank, then went to French's Store and to the Forest House to get more guns. He gave one to William Maw and kept one for himself. The two went to the alley behind the Forest House and stopped at the entrance of Howard and Reynold's store, where Maw remained.

Holman, meanwhile, went through the alley along the Vienna Bakery to Metcalf Street. He crossed the street and continued through the alley alongside Condy's Jewelry Shop to the vacant lots east of the brick building which faced the rear of the Wixson Hotel and the First National Bank. From that position, he fired five shots toward the bandits at the rear of the bank.

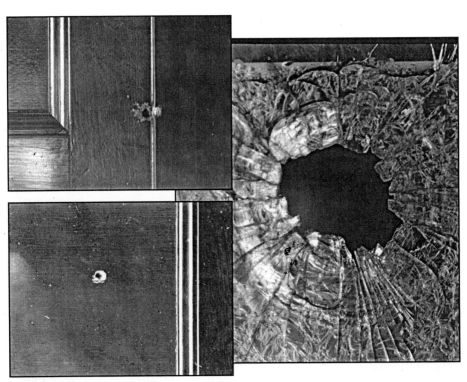

Where several shots was fired through this partition at cashier. Fifty-two shots were fired from the interior of the Bank, after their guns were emptied another bandit entered from the rear breaking open the back door, covering bank Officers with his guns. Forcing Cashier, Book-keeper and assistant cashier into the back room where they all gathered at the Vault.

Beebe, who was at the Bingham Bank when the shooting began, was given a Winchester rifle from Mr. Bingham before running toward the First National Bank. He stopped in front of the barber shop in the Vienna Bakery building and emptied both the rifle and an automatic, which he had in his pocket – 16 shots in all. He then ran back for more ammunition.

Unfortunately, Beebe's shots spoiled plans for one good samaritan. Mr. A.J. Morrison, an ex-sheriff who was staying in the Wixson Hotel at the time, borrowed a gun from the night clerk and ran across the street, ducking bullets. Crouching down behind a car directly across the street from the bank, he had perfect aim at the outlaws. But after quickly using the only three bullets in the gun without hitting the bandits, and with Beebe firing down the street, Morrison had no way of getting to the extra ammunition from the hotel clerk, and was forced to retreat.

Another attempt to kill the robbers was foiled for a local attorney, Mr. Cogswell, not due to another person's actions, but his own lack of experience with guns. He had borrowed an automatic from a nearby billiards room, as the clerk informed him that he just needed to aim and pull the trigger. Cogswell crossed the street to Mott's Drug Store and attempted to shoot. The safety was on the gun, and by the time he figured out what the problem was, the bandits had escaped.

While the robbery was playing out, a frightened telephone exchange operator had locked herself inside her office adjoining the Wixson Café. She made a frantic call to Sheriff Ed Wells in Mount Vernon. "Listen to them shooting," she cried. She then held the receiver out so they could clearly hear the shots on the other end. Wells immediately left in his car for Sedro-Woolley.

Narrowly escaping death in the shootout were Mr. Mott, the druggist, and Dr. Fred Mills, who were both inside Mott's Drug Store. After hearing the first shots, Mott ran to the back door of his establishment to see what the commotion was. Just as he got there, he realized that he was being shot at, and quickly retreated. Mills, meanwhile, had shut off the lights and stood by a window to watch the action. But like Mott, he also quickly put his curiosity aside when a bullet crashed through the window just above his head.

Thirteen-year-old Melvin Wilson wasn't so lucky. The young son of Mr. and Mrs. James Wilson, heard the shots outside and said to his mother, "Oh, Mama, hear the shooting." He then immediately ran out of their house near the bank, and to the Northern Pacific tracks about a block north. He started towards the bank when a bullet struck him in the abdomen, according to later news reports "entering in front, high up above the groin and to the right of the left hip, passing straight through." Young Melvin would be the only fatality in the shootout.

Mrs. Margaret "Maggie" Osterman lived just behind the bank on Ferry Street and had a great view of the action. Her daughter Suzie lived half a block from her mother's house, and had just started to walk there when the shooting began. She quickly retreated to safety just in time. Maggie had been watching the robbery through a window facing downtown, and had just stepped away from it when it was shot out.

Father, Mother and Sister of little Melvin Wilson, who lost his life on the night of October the 17th. Little Melvin Wilson at the time the robbery started was at his home directly across the street. Not even stopping to get his hat, he rushed out, and his Mother seeing him go out the door, little thought it would be the last time she would see her son alive.

Little Melvin Wilson, crossed the street to the Rail Road Track, still thinking that it was merely sport he started toward the bank and a bullet from one of the bandits gun stopped his young career.

Spot showing where Melvin Wilson was shot.

Also with a good view of the robbery was a young newsboy from the Bellingham Herald, "Pike" Pilcher. Pike was very close to the bank and started running down the street when he realized what was happening. In his excitement, though, he tripped over a rack of lawn tools. Realizing he was likely safer on the ground than standing, he stayed where he was until the gunfire ended. "It had the German War backed off the map," he would later tell the newspaper.

The robbers stationed behind the bank kicked in the back door of the building. They continued through bank president Wixson's personal office and into the bank, firing shots at Guddall as they entered. One of the men got close enough to shove his gun into Guddall's ribs. The Skagit Times later reported, "John reflected upon all the possibilities of life, and his hands ascended a considerable bit nearer heaven."

Guddall tried to stall the robbers by telling them that the safe was on a timed lock. They realized, though that he was lying and jabbed their guns further into his sides. One pushed a gun into Guddall's back "so far that the muzzle seemed to be in his vest pocket," he later said.

Back door which leader of bandits kicked in to give assistance to his comrades.

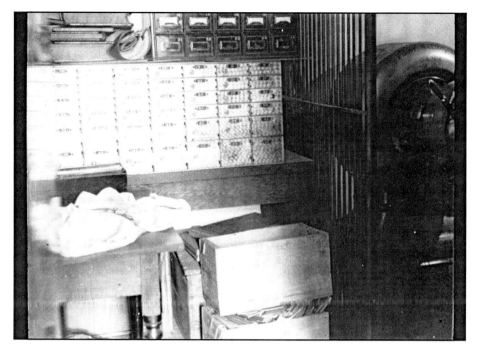

Mr. Guddall attempted to tell them that it was a time lock; they answered him that they knew better and that he had better open it up. Therefore forcing Mr. Guddall to open the vault and pass out the bags containing money.

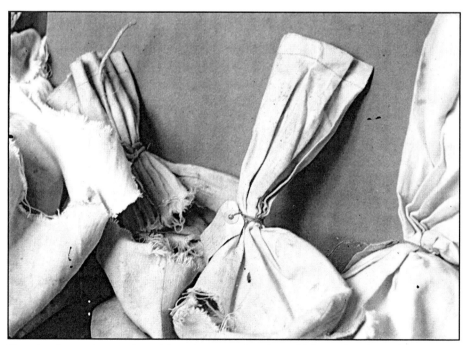

Showing bags cut open by robbers in separating the gold from the silver, then passing through the back door of the bank out into the night.

Guddall, knowing that he could no longer hold the men off, finally relented and opened the vault. The bandits opened the bags of coins, leaving most of the ones containing silver. Bags of gold coins were placed under each arm of the robbers. As there weren't enough bags of gold for all of the men, one man reluctantly took the silver ones. They also reportedly took much of the paper money from the bank.

After taking what they had come for, the robbers inside the bank joined their two companions outside. They ran down the street, firing behind them as they went. They ran east on Ferry Street to Murdock Street, passing by Mrs. Osterman's home. She watched them continue north on Murdock Street until they were out of sight. She later reported that they were speaking a foreign language and that none of them appeared to have been wounded, despite all the gunfire. Sheriff Wells would later theorize the men were Russians who were part of a larger gang that had been suspected of numerous recent robberies throughout Washington State and Canada.

It was first believed that the bandits had fled in an automobile, but Sheriff Wells who arrived at the scene just minutes after the robbers left, could not find any evidence to back up that claim.

After having left Maw at Howard and Reynold's store, Marshal Villeneuve had crossed the street to the rear of the Wixson Hotel, but when he got to the front of the building, the robbers had already fled. Likewise, after running back for more ammunition, Rolly Beebe returned to find that he was too late as well.

Fearing further gunfire, none of Sedro-Woolley's police officers tried to immediately follow the bandits. A posse was formed by Wells, including numerous volunteers from Mount Vernon and Burlington. In all, over 100 men searched through the woods along the railroad tracks north of town that night, but had no luck locating the criminals. A few suspicious men were questioned in the area, but all of them had credible alibis. Officers considered obtaining the closest bloodhound dogs available, which were in the town of Monroe, but they later determined that the chance of them finding a scent might be minimal, considering the heavy rains that deluged the area just after the robbery.

Sheriff Wells, of Skagit Co., who was in Sedro-Woolley an hour after the robbery occured and who never left the scene until the capture of the Bandits.

Side view of the bank, showing a telephone pole at the rear of the bank directly across the street from the rear of Mr. Mott's Drug Store by which one of the bandits stood. Eleven clips were found on the ground, each clip had contained nine cartridges, showing that ninety nine shots had been fired from this place.

Showing destruction of big plate glass in front of bank.

Showing destruction of windows at close range.

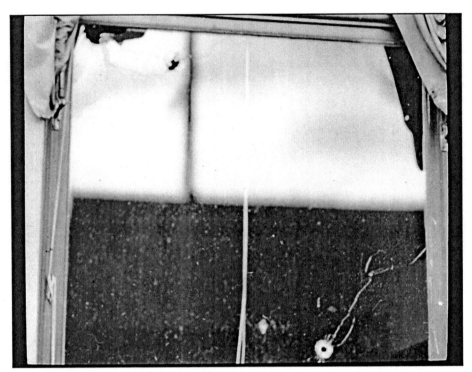

Showing destruction of windows at close range.

Back of chair with bullet lodged in same.

View showing broken glass-door in President Wixson's private Office.

Showing Damage done to President Wixson's $3,000.00 car.

Showing windows of the Union Mercantile Co., Directly across the street, which was completely destroyed during the battle, over $300.00 damage done to this store.

Mr. Jack Barick, Clerk of the union Mercantile Co. Standing in the exact position as he was on the night of the robbery, showing bullet hole a few inches from his head, driving him inside.

Showing another shot taken at Jack while getting into the Store.

The window of a private residence; through which a bullet passed, lodging in a picture frame, which barely missed the mistress of the house.

Showing damage done to hard-ware Store Opposite the bank.

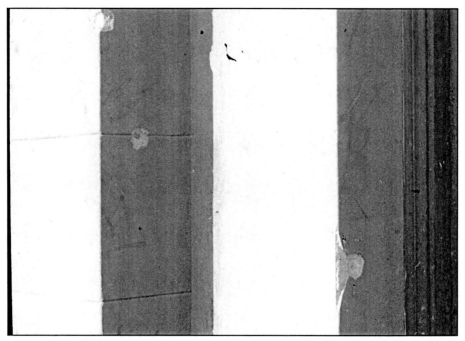

Bullet holes in concrete outside the bank where officers attempted to get bandits.

The back street down which the bandits took after making their haul, passing out over this Rail Road.

The railroad at that time was under construction but since has been completed. At that time there were four Hundred men working on this road. Four miles down this road they entered the forest, this forest being dense and impenetrable, to where the camp was located.

3

The Aftermath

The daylight of Sunday morning brought a devastating sight to the citizens of Sedro-Woolley. Their downtown businesses and homes were splintered and shattered. Shot out windows had been boarded up, and there were holes in most of the walls of the nearby buildings. In all, an estimated 200 shots had been fired in the duration of 10 to 15 minutes that the shootout took place, and $11,649.45 was taken. Inside the bank, bullets were lodged in a typewriter and adding machine, among other damage. Some drops of blood were discovered in the bank, backing a claim by Guddall that he shot one of the men. The wound appeared only minor, though, as no blood was found outside.

Beginning Sunday morning, posses scoured the forests and highways from Sedro-Woolley north to Canada. No clues were found until the morning of Tuesday, October 20, when it was reported that a posse of four men discovered two bandits in the hills seven miles from town. One of the men was reportedly wounded, and another was left to take care of him. They were said to have been covered with some boughs over a hollow stump and were aware that they had been discovered. However, the news later turned out to not have merit, and the men were not seen again.

Another false lead occurred when Sedro-Woolley resident Bert Ingham and a male Northern State Hospital employee were hunting for the robbers during early morning hours. The hospital worker reported smelling something similar to Idoform, a disinfectant that may have been used on wounds suffered by one of the bandits. The two men noted their location and returned to town for help. A posse was quickly formed and driven in three cars to the area the two men had been. They walked to the exact area, where the posse members also smelled it. They quickly turned back, however, after discovering the smell was actually coming from a common weed in the forest with a similar fragrance.

Their camp consisted of a natural abode. Protected from all sides by wind falls. Showing smooth places on the logs where they had slid over them in coming and going from camp, and showing the camp had been inhabited. Between the logs was covered with dry moss, the farther and covered with small wind-falls where they slept. These black places show where they had their fires.

Look-out tree showing the seat at the base of the tree, where a constant look-out was kept upon the Rail Road, twigs being broken away for about three hundred yards, so this view could be obtained. This camp was accidently found by a Hunter who immediately reported it to the police. The police going to this camp found evidence and maps to the effect that they had probably been there for four or five weeks.

An abandoned camp was also found four miles north of Sedro-Woolley on the Whatcom-Skagit county line between Thornwood and Prairie. A group of searchers found pieces of an apron torn into strips and stained with blood, which was believed to have been used as a bandage for the outlaw who was wounded in the gunfight, but no further leads from the evidence were discovered.

The Bellingham Herald on October 20, 1914, reported that a possible clue to the route that the robbers took was found when a car stolen from Milltown was found in Seattle. While the idea that the men got away in a vehicle was considered, it was later determined to not be likely.

On Wednesday, October 21, the search for the bandits intensified in Whatcom County after Immigration Inspector Thomas Wyckoff was threatened by three men in Ferndale. He met the men as they were walking north along the Great Northern Railroad tracks at 2:45 a.m. He told them who he was and asked them to follow him to the depot 300 yards away so he could get a better look at them. They followed his instructions without resistance, but when they got to the depot platform,

Sheriff Thomas, of Whatcom County who followed the bandits to their final capture.

all of the men pulled out their large revolvers and held them to Wyckoff's stomach.

"I guess you don't want us," one of the men reportedly said. "We know where we're going and you're not going to stop us." Wyckoff retreated and the three men were joined by two others from the bushes before heading further north out of sight.

Following this sighting of the presumed suspects, Sheriffs L.A. Thomas and Ed Wells alerted all law enforcement agencies in the area with circulars asking them to investigate any suspects matching their descriptions. The circulars described the men as "foreigners, most-likely Russians, dark, resembling Greeks. One six feet tall, others from five feet, five inches to five feet, eight inches, stocky."

Wells, Thomas, and Deputy Wilson Stewart of Whatcom County also headed up small posses of armed men to the area between Ferndale and Blaine to try to prevent the men from crossing over into Canada. The farmers in the area were also alerted and joined in the search.

Tom L. Wyckoff, U.S. Immigrant Inspector stationed at Ferndale, Wn.

Showing the road which they took passing through Blaine, the old and new G.N.R.R. (Great Northern Railroad)

A view showing where they passed through Blaine.

After a reported sighting later Wednesday of the five men going north from Wickersham on the Northern Pacific tracks, Wells and his deputies searched around the town of Deming, but found no evidence that they were in the area. That night, Deming Chief of Police Al Callahan and a posse guarded Nugent's Bridge, assuming that the men would eventually cross it if they were in the area. They returned home the next morning, however, reporting that they were likely on a "wild clue".

Thursday, October 22 at 3:00 a.m., the gang finally arrived at the US/Canadian border and made an attempt to cross it. Frank McDowell and Leo Hyde were on guard and ordered the men to halt. The men ran, however, and escaped ensuing gunfire from the guards. At 3:30 a.m., the five bandits were spotted by Canadian Officer Cliff Adams, American Immigration Officer A.E. Burke, and Great Northern Detective E.H. Keith at the North Bluff Crossing near Hazelmere, B.C., where a wagon road intersected the old Great Northern Railroad tracks. The outlaws were ordered to halt, but resisted. A gun fight broke out, during which Adams was shot through the heart, killing him instantly.

View showing where the robbers passed through Blaine, ducking under the Electric light in a crouching position about twenty feet apart as seen by Deputy Phillip Shaffner, who reported them to the Officers in Blaine, who attempted to head them off before they got into Canada, but were too late.

Showing scene on old G.N.R.R. (Great Northern Railroad line) that robbers took just before crossing the boundary line.

Douglass Station at Boundary Line where Deputies Hide and McDonald were stationed, but owing to the darkness and the precaution which the bandits took, they got by the Deputies before being noticed, the signal alarm was given by firing six shots in quick Succession there-by warning all the Deputies on both sides, that the Bandits had passed into Canada.

View of Deputies Hide and Frank McDonald

Looking East on the Boundary line, and about two miles in distance from the Douglass Station lies the old Chinese or Smugglers trail, this vicinity was heavily guarded by Sheriffs and Deputies on this night.

Scene on the old G.N. line where the first bloody battle took place, resulting in the loss of three lives and two wounded.

Thicket where robbers concealed them-selves before the battle.

Keith was shot through the hand, and Burke's hat was hit by a bullet as well. One of the bandits was killed in the gunfight, and one was hit in the hip. Upon witnessing the casualties, the remaining three suspects quickly left. They continued north, followed soon by a posse of at least 200 men from Blaine and the surrounding areas.

An hour after the fight near Hazelmere, B.C., Sheriffs Wells and Thomas found the wounded robber near the railroad tracks. He was unconscious and had a bullet hole through the back of his head. Initially, it was assumed that the man had shot himself. However, later it was determined that one of the man's companions must have shot him, considering the wound was in the back of the head.

The whole story of the gunfight at Hazelmere was later told by Mr. Keith in an interview with the Bellingham Herald printed on October 23, 1914:

> *"Suddenly a voice was heard by our party. We shouted to them to 'come on out and surrender.' Our only answer was a perfect volley of shot that blazed wickedly in our faces. Again and again, shot followed shot in each rapid succession as to seem like one prolonged volley. We returned the fire.*

Spot showing where the Pok-marked bandit was found dead.

"Hidden as they were behind a 12-foot embankment, they had us at a disadvantage. Not a word spoken to break the uncanny stillness. Silently, Inspector Adams fell, mortally wounded. A bullet hit me in the hand in which I held the gun, and I rolled over the opposite embankment.

"Thinking us both dead, Inspector Burke, with his own gun emptied, gave up the fight and fled back for reinforcements. From my concealed place, I saw two of the robbers helping a third down the tracks. He seemed to be badly hurt, and a fourth bandit followed the three along, keeping under cover of the embankment, and ready to protect the other three from assailants.

"I knew they had left one of their number behind, as he filled the air with terrible moans and curses.

"I managed to make away to a nearby logging camp, where they gave my hand what attention they could. The bullet had passed through my little finger and through my wrist.

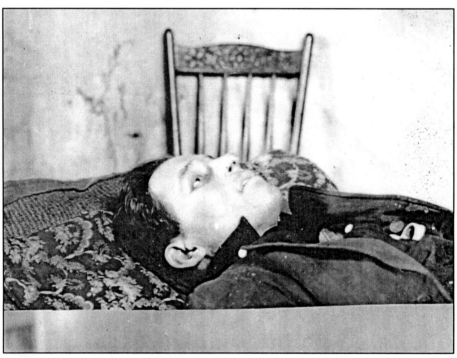

A good View of the Pok-marked bandit.

This shows where Clifford Adams fell after being shot through the heart.

Clifford Adams, the very promising young man, in the immigration services of Canada, a good clean man in every respect, liked by all his associates, and a brave and fearless man as ever worked for any Government. He gave his life in the performance of his duty.

"Hearing the Sheriff's force approaching, I again joined them. We found one man dead lying on the ground at the scene of the fight. Two belts were about his person, containing about $3,000 in gold. He wore one about his shoulders and one around his waist. He also had three automatic revolvers in his belt and was evidently the gang leader.

"About a quarter of a mile further down the track, we came upon another bandit, breathing at last. I suppose he was the wounded man they were assisting as their forms were swallowed up in the darkness from my viewpoint in the ditch. The dying man had evidently just been shot in the head, either by himself or by one of his companions, and life fled as we watched. He had $200 in silver tied up in his handkerchief."

The dead and mortally wounded bandits were placed together in a wagon and taken to Cloverdale, British Columbia. It was determined that the two men were likely the ringleaders of the larger gang. The total amount recovered from the two bandits was $3,067.20.

This spot shows where the second bandit was found wounded about one quarter of a mile from the scene of the battle, shot once through the hip at the battle at the R.R. crossing and later was shot in the head by one of his fellow-men, when unable to keep up with them any longer, he lived thirty-six hours after being found.

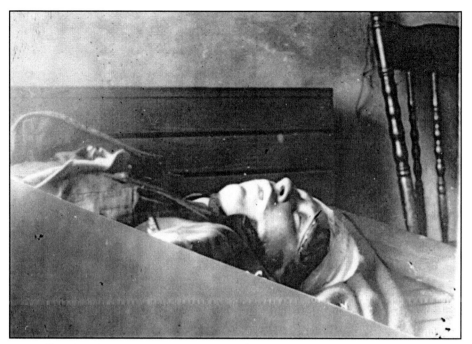

View of bandit who was shot by his pals.

Turning the camera around and standing on the track where the first battle took place and about thirty-five feet distance, is where some six years ago, Mrs. Morrison was murdered, having her throat cut from ear to ear by a Mulatto who made his escape afterward. He was caught, convicted and hung at New Westminster, B.C.

Charcoal drawing of the first robber who was killed, the "Pok-marked bandit".

SEDRO-WOLLEY

ALLEN'S ORIGINAL
B. R. S.

BANK ROBBER and BANDIT ESLAN JISELOFF
WHO WAS SUPPOSED TO HAVE BEEN SHOT BY HIS
PARDNERS WHEN NOT ABLE TO KEEP UP AFTER RECEI
VING A WOUND IN THE FIGHT NEAR HAZELMERE B.C.

Charcoal drawing of the second killed robber who was shot in the head by another robber.

Spot showing G.N. Detective Keefe after being wounded in the gun hand.

Team, wagon and driver, who conveyed the bodies of the bandits to the jail at Cloverdale, B.C.

A group of U.S. and Canadian Officers in front of the jail at Cloverdale, B.C.

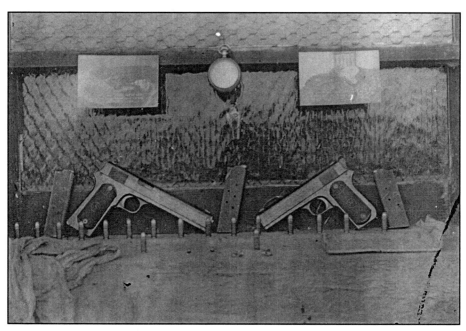

Bullets, clips, and cartridges, watch and chain that was taken from the bandits. By noticing very closely you will notice that the charm on the watch-chain is a miniture Revolver thus showing you in what way their minds run.

Burning the clothes of the bandits at Cloverdale, B.C.

Hat showing bullet hole. This hat was worn by U.S. Inspector Burke which shows the narrow escape he had from loosing his life.

Deputies from U.S. guarding the high-ways near Cloverdale, B.C.

Mr Brock Jr., Deputy of Bellingham.

Mr. Barney Hanson, of Blaine Deputized for the reason that he knew every foot of the roads and trails in and around the International border.

Showing how they guarded every fence corner and by-trail.

U.S. and Canadian Deputies with blood-hounds searching the forest for the bandits trail.

Showing how skid-roads and high-ways was guarded on the day after the shooting, near Hazelmere, B.C.

4

Hunt for the Final Three

On Friday, October 23, it became apparent that the three remaining bandits had crossed the border and were once again in the United States. They were spotted in a field near Blaine owned by "Farmer McGee", a black man who had just been leaving on his way home. McGee saw the three men and waited for them to come closer so he could talk to them. They asked the way to the town of Custer, and then carried on a casual conversation for five minutes before leaving. McGee realized that the men were most likely the bandits who had been headlining the local news, and reported the encounter to the authorities.

Farmer McGee who saw and talked to the bandits, he leaving the field to go to the house for his noon-day meal, noticing three men coming down the road, he lingered at the gate to have a talk with them, but they also wished to talk to him stopped and asked the way to Custer, carrying on an ordinary conversation for at least five minutes. All this time Farmer McGee was Closely scrutinizing their Countenance, dress and appearance and coming to the conclusion that they were the bandits notified the authorities.

Farmer McGee and his boys showing the road they took after leaving McGee's farm.

Mr. McGee, is a highly respected colored gentleman, having lived in the vicinity of Blaine for some years. Previous to his residence near Blaine he was U.S. Deputy Marshall for nine years in Mobile Co., Alabama.

Mrs. Otto Wilson, the wife of a nearby farmer, also reported an encounter with the bandits. She was alone in her home eight miles north of Ferndale, when at 7:30 a.m., three "rough looking men" arrived. They ordered the frightened lady to give them food, so she obliged with six loaves of bread and two rolls of butter. They ordered her to stay inside her house until noon, shouting threats to her as they were leaving. At noon, Mrs. Wilson ran to a neighbor's house and reported the incident. The sheriff's office was immediately notified and security in the area was significantly increased as the officers anticipated that the suspects would pass through Ferndale on the Great Northern tracks that evening.

Authorities were thoroughly prepared for the arrival of the bandits in Ferndale as night fell. A headlight from Sheriff Wells' Ford car was cleverly connected to six dry cell batteries and attached to a block building that the deputies had hastily constructed on one side of the Great Northern bridge over the Nooksack River at Ferndale. The light could be switched on if the bandits crossed the bridge, blinding them and giving authorities a chance to capture or shoot them.

The home of Mrs. Wilson, the house where the men stopped after Fatigue and Hunger had forced them to show them-selves to civilization, rapping at the door of Mrs. Wilson. They asked for food but not having any meat in the house, she gave them six loaves of bread and two rolls of butter. Then telling her to go into the house and warned her not to come out again until 12:00 O-Clock, this taking place at 8:00 O-Clock in the Morning.

View of Mrs. Wilson, the kind Lady who fed the Bandits.

Sheriff Wells and his Automobile that were hot on the Bandits trail from start to finish. The light of this Automobile was the one used at Ferndale, to light the bridge over which the bandits tried to pass.

Maurice Dean, Electrician of Blaine who arranged the light on the R.R. bridge at Ferndale.

A group of Deputies that were on the bandits trail under Sheriff Wells of Skagit County, reading from left to right, Bradley, Jack Taylor, Game Warden Elkins, and Charley Stevenson.

This gives a good view of the old Chinese or Smugglers Trail.

Showing the route which the bandits took in returning to the United States. Passing through the old Chinese or Smugglers Trail, which was so heavily guarded the night before but clear the following day.

Powder house near Blaine where bandits stopped over night.

The Bridge crossing the river at Ferndale, where Mr. Wells and his Deputies being stationed on each side of the river.

Late Friday night, Deputy Stewart, Ferndale Fire Chief Fred Roessel, and two private detectives were on guard at the bridge. At about 11:30 p.m., two of the men decided to take a break. While walking around, one of them stepped in a cold puddle. He asked the other man to accompany him to the building to dry off. The bandits, who had been watching the guards, waited for them to go inside, then started across the bridge on their hands and knees. They were approximately 20 feet from the other side of the bridge when they were heard. The rigged light was switched on, causing them great frustration. Going for their guns, they were ordered to halt by Roessel. They didn't stop, however, so Roessel fired and hit one man. Stewart then shot the other. One man was later found to have had a charge of buckshot enter his side and exit through his chest. The other was shot in the head. The Bellingham Herald the following day reported that he "lived for about an hour and a half after being wounded, although part of the back of his head had been torn away." The two dead bandits were ten feet apart on the bridge.

A view of the R.R. bridge a few yards further up the river guarded by Sheriff Thomas, Deputy Sheriff Stewart and others from Whatcom County.

Deputy Roselle who took a very important part in the capture of the bandits at Ferndale.

A close View of Deputy Roselle.

Deputy Conklin, who was also very prominent in the capture of the bandits at Ferndale.

The shed where the men (deputies) stood one or two hours before the bandits crossed.

The bandits had reached with-in about twenty feet of the other side when discovered. They were promptly ordered to hault, failing to obay they were given one more chance. HAULT. Bang, Bang, Bang, Bang!

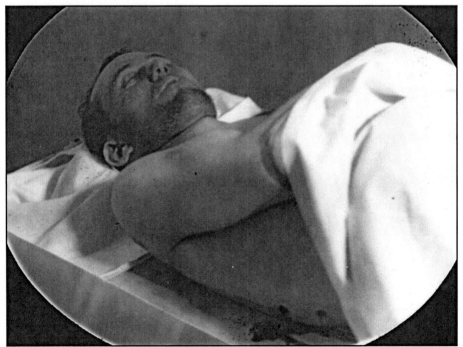

Showing one of the bandits Killed, a charge of Buck-shot entering in his left side and coming through his breast.

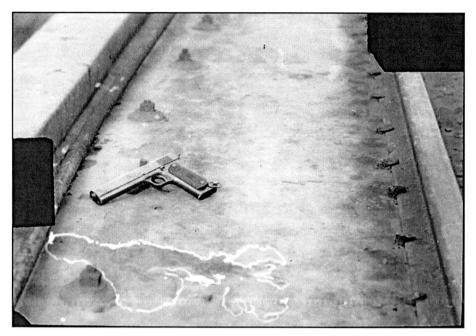

Showing the spot where the two Bandits fell about ten feet apart, the tallest being shot in the head, spots showing stains of blood.

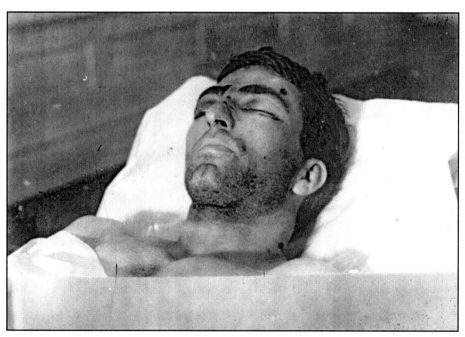

Showing the other bandit which was shot in the head with a charge of Buck-shot also, but still lived an hour and twenty minutes after. This man was a most perfect muscled man, his muscles on his body as you can see large and numerous, his physical strength being equal to a half dozen ordinary men.

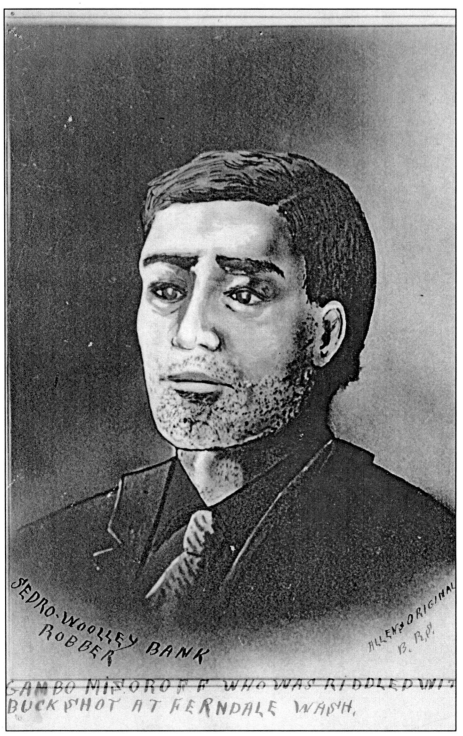

Charcoal drawing of the first robber killed in Ferndale, WA.

Charcoal drawing of the second robber killed in Ferndale, WA.

The third bandit had been some distance behind the other two, and had a chance to escape. J.J. Carpenter, a man who lived near the railroad tracks, heard the shots and looked outside, later claiming to have seen the third bandit running towards the river.

Following the Ferndale shootout, Deputy Coroner R.B. Stuart of Whatcom County was called to the scene where the men died, and arrived at 2:00 a.m. He ordered the bodies to be taken to A.G. Wickman's Undertaking Parlors in Bellingham. After word got around that the two dead bandits from the Ferndale shootout were with Wickman, hundreds of people came to view the corpses. They were lying out on cold slabs, bullet wounds clearly visible.

People curiously examined the men and thoroughly discussed them. The short man was dark with heavy black hair, and was reported to have features that were "clearly Slavic". The taller one, with lighter hair, had features of an American, but it was believed that he was foreign also – Russian or Polish. The men wore hats, logging boots, and heavy flannel shirts. All tags showing where their clothing had been purchased were removed, although there were marks on the coats that indicated they may have been from Seattle. No identification was found on the men. The short one had a hole in his forehead and another between the right eye and ear, coming out of the forehead and causing his eye to bulge out. Another shot had penetrated his neck. The larger man had four buckshot holes in the right side of his back. The taller of the two dead bandits had $55 in currency, $54.45 in silver, and $1,435 in gold, totaling $1,544.45. The other man had $35 in currency, $28.65 in silver, and $1,480 in gold, totaling $1,543.65. The total value found with the men in the Ferndale shootout was $3,088.10.

After viewing the bodies of the dead bandits, many people claimed to have known or seen the men at various times before or after the bank robbery in Sedro-Woolley. L. McKenzie, who operated a cigar stand on Elk Street in Bellingham, said the taller man had been in his store three days earlier. Mr. L.C. Short, who owned a store in Silver Beach, also said the man had purchased six loaves of bread and some sausage from his store the same day. Short did not report the man at the time, however, as he had given a "straight story", saying he was on his way to Clear Lake.

Another sighting was by Jerry Rogers, a bricklayer, who said the tall bandit had worked for him in Mount Vernon not long before the robbery. Mail carrier Francis Corey reported that she had been delivering mail to the short man at a Greek-operated pool room on West Holly Street in Bellingham. She claimed his name was George Pappas, and he resided in New Westminster, B.C., where he operated a cigar stand. Chancey Cissna also identified the man as Pappas on Saturday afternoon, saying he was the former proprietor of the Depot Restaurant on West Holly Street in Bellingham. Joe Peters also identified him, adding that he had a wife and five children. The identifications of the man as George Pappas were later determined to be incorrect.

Cashier Guddall, Matt Kakko, Homer Shrewsbury, and W.H. Curry viewed all four dead bandits on Saturday morning and identified them as the men who had robbed the Sedro-Woolley bank. Guddall said the man shot near Hazelmere was the one who had kicked in the back door of the bank building. He also said the one identified as Pappas had been in his bank several times prior to the robbery to cash checks.

After identifying the men at the undertaking parlors, the men from Sedro-Woolley along with Sheriff Wells continued on to Cloverdale, B.C. where two suspects were held. One of the suspects gave his name as D. Danzaloff. Canadian detectives had been investigating him for nearly a month, as it had been reported to them that the man had no job, but had an unusually large amount of money. A search of his home had found a large supply of guns and ammunition. Guddall could not positively identify either man, but Danzaloff remained in custody for further investigation. "Although neither Mr. Guddall or myself were able to identify the suspect as being one of the men connected directly with the Sedro-Woolley robbery, we both think that there is reason to believe that he is implicated," said Sheriff Ed Wells in a later interview. "He tallies closely with the men of the band that I saw after they had been killed. (Canadian) authorities are sure that he is a bad one."

Numerous Canadian officials went to view the corpses, as the dead men had been suspects in many other robberies throughout Canada. The officials included Provincial Police Inspector Wynn; A. D. Matheson, Chief Constable of Surrey; D. Matheson, Deputy Constable of Surrey;

and F.J. MacKenzie, Provincial Member of Parliament. Wynn said he would compare fingerprints of the men with those found on the various crime scenes before making any statements. The Canadian officers, however, said they were sure the men were part of a large gang which had operated in Canada.

On Sunday, October 24, the Bellingham Herald reported, "Today the entire Nooksack Valley is watching for the fifth bandit, and it is believed that he has little chance of escaping." In the law enforcement community, Sheriff Thomas borrowed a bloodhound from Mr. James Hawkins, but turned up no trails. Sheriff Wells and Deputy Stewart stood guard at the ferry at Marietta, but found no trace of the bandit. Many posses formed throughout the region with a focus around Lynden, and Sheriff Thomas deputized dozens of men to take part in the hunt.

On Sunday, October 25, a potential suspect, Henry Leiver who identified himself as a Bohemian, was arrested following a purchase of bread at Roush's Confectionery Store on Harris Avenue near Chuckanut Bay in Bellingham. He had asked a boy who was playing at the beach to buy $1 worth of bread for him. The boy became suspicious and ran away, however, so Leiver went to the store himself. He purchased coffee and doughnuts, and then asked to buy five loaves of bread. William Small, who was in the store at the same time and had suspicions about Leiver, notified authorities. Nearly a mile south of the store, Leiver was arrested by Officer Harry Jordan. Leiver had little money, but the skin around his waist and across one shoulder looked worn as though he had been carrying heavy money belts similar to the ones used by the bank robbers.

Leiver told police he had walked to Bellingham from Seattle, having departed Burlington on Sunday. The officers theorized, though, that Leiver had paid someone to row him from the Nooksack River near Marietta to the place where he was seen near Chuckanut Bay. Then, they suspected, he hid his gun and money in the woods. Despite Leiver's arrest, the search continued since the evidence was not conclusive. Leiver was close in appearance to the robbers in the Ferndale gunfight. He had a similar beard and his clothes were worn. Officers said he looked like he could very well have been a brother to one of the dead robbers. On the contrary, Mrs. Wilson, the woman who gave the bandits bread before the fight in Ferndale, said Leiver had lighter skin than the suspects she had seen. Also, she said, his clothes were different. Leiver wore a Mackinaw coat, which he claimed he had purchased in Spokane two weeks prior. He also wore bicycle shoes, which authorities believed he had purchased on the Lummi Indian Reservation.

On Monday, October 26, George Pappas, the man once believed to have been one of the dead robbers, arrived in Bellingham from New Westminster to clear his name. Those who saw him admitted that they had made a mistake, though there was consensus that he resembled one of the dead men. Later, H.H. Emerson, a telephone company employee, said the bandit who had falsely been identified as Pappas, had worked for him as a powderman in Haynie, B.C., two years earlier, but had been fired for continually being "drunk and quarrelsome"

Deputy Stewart arrived at the Whatcom County courthouse Monday afternoon, October 26, with the money taken from the bandits killed in Ferndale. The money was turned over to the coroner to be kept until its owner was determined. The money, by law, was to be held by the coroner for 30 days, and then turned over to the county treasurer who was to hold it for six years. If unclaimed, the money would have been turned over to the State's school fund. The Sedro-Woolley bank was protected by insurance, so it was believed that they would not claim the money. The money taken from the bandits killed in Canada remained in the hands of Canadian officials.

The two bandits killed in Ferndale were buried the afternoon of October 27, at the Potter's Field in the Bayview Cemetery in Bellingham. Their true identity remains unknown, and their graves were left unmarked.

The burial location of the two robbers killed in Hazelmere, BC is unknown as of the printing of this book.

Whatcom County, Washington.

CORONER'S REGISTER.

Name of Deceased...*Unknown*... Date of Inquest...*Oct 24*... 19*14*

Name of place where Inquest was held...

Description of locality where body was found *on G. Northern Ry Bridge at Ferndale Wash*

DESCRIPTION WHEN NAME OF DECEASED IS NOT KNOWN:

Age *about 38 yrs* Height *5 ft 9½ in* Eyes... Hair...

Beard *none* Moustache... Complexion *light*

Weight *about 181* Kind and Color of Clothes...

NAMES OF JURORS	JURORS PER DIEM	NAMES OF WITNESSES
		Reported by American Reveille Office
		Witnesses
		Wilson Clement
		Fred Rozelle
		Fred Dean

CORONER'S FEES		FINDINGS OF JURY AS TO CAUSE OF DEATH
Subpœnas		*The deceased was one of a number of robbers*
Summons		*who looted a Sedro Woolley bank and was shot*
Transcripts		*to death by officers of the law while attempting*
Oaths		*to cross the Ry bridge at Ferndale Wash*
Mileage		
Filing Papers		DISPOSITION OF BODY
Per Diem		*Buried by Workman*

DESCRIPTION OF PERSONAL EFFECTS

DISPOSITION OF PERSONAL EFFECTS

Dr H Thompson
Co Coroner

REMARKS

Coroner's Register from the burial of one of the two robbers. Text from above: "The deceased is one of a number of robbers who looted a Sedro-Woolley bank and was shot to death by officers of the law while attempting to cross the railroad bridge at Ferndale, Wash.

CORONER'S REGISTER.

Name of Deceased _Unknown_   Date of Inquest _Oct 24_ 19_14_

Name of place where Inquest was held _____

Description of locality where body was found _on Gt Northern Ry Bridge Ferndale Wash_

DESCRIPTION WHEN NAME OF DECEASED IS NOT KNOWN:

Age _about 35_   Height _5 ft 6 in_   Eyes _____   Hair _____

Beard _none_   Moustache _____   Complexion _dark_

Weight _about 175_   Kind and Color of Clothes _____

NAMES OF JURORS	JURORS PER DIEM	NAMES OF WITNESSES
		Wilson Sawant
		Fred Trouble
		Fred Dean

CORONER'S FEES	FINDINGS OF JURY AS TO CAUSE OF DEATH
Subpœnas · · ·	The deceased was one of a number of officers who tried to get a trolley car and was shot to death by Sergt. of the law while attempting to cross the Ry bridge at Ferndale Wash
Summons · · ·	
Transcripts · ·	
Oaths · · · ·	
Mileage · · · ·	DISPOSITION OF BODY
Filing Papers ·	Buried by Wickman
Per Diem · · ·	

DESCRIPTION OF PERSONAL EFFECTS

DISPOSITION OF PERSONAL EFFECTS

Dr H Thompson
Co Coroner

REMARKS

October   Term   Tuesday   the   8th day   December   1914

Tuesday, December 8, 1914. The Board met pursuant to adjournment taken on December 7, 1914. Present, all members of the Board and the Clerk in attendance. The following claims were allowed and proceedings had:

CURRENT EXPENSE FUND.

P G Cooke	Expense as Deputy Co Engineer	10.80
O N Munn	do (Russell Ditch)	8.50
Harrison Cowden	Expense as Constable	2.00
O E Beebe	Expense as Co Physician a/c Convention in Seattle	8.80
C C King	Expense as Supt Co Home	36.83
W J Pynor	Groceries & Powder etc for Co Home	226.70
Wilson, Nobles, Barr Co	Groceries for Co Home	111.07
Royal Dairy Co	Butter for Co Home	53.20
Anton Anderson	Beef for Co Home	27.90
Geo Casebeer	Grinding feed for Co Home	4.40
Battersby Bros.	Clothing etc for Co Home	46.57
B B Furniture Co	Mattress etc for Co Home	3.50
Northwest Hdw. Co	Utensils etc for Co Home	9.10
Morse Hdw. Co	do	5.65
M G Kelly	Repairs to Plumbing at Co Home	2.00
T W Suckling	Blacksmithing for Co Home	15.25
Dr H A Compton	Assisting Co Physician	10.00
Dr F A Wheaton	do	10.00
Dr E C Ruge	do	20.00
St Luke's Hospital	Care of Co Patients	176.00
St Joseph's Hospital	do	122.56
The Weiser Drug Co	Medicine for Co Patients	7.75
Red Cross Pharmacy	do	15.55
Collins & Co	do	7.15
E Edson	Medicine for Co Patients	12.95
Pacific Wasserman Labratories	Blood test for Co Patient	5.00
Mrs A Graveline	Board of Wm Mapley	32.20
Mellie Petersen	Care of Mrs Bjorndahl	30.00
Pacific Tel & Tel Co	Rentals for December	37.25
do	Long Distance for November	11.60
Western Union Telg. Co	Messages for Sher 1.49 & Supt .50	1.99
Postal Tel-Cable Co	Messages for Probation Officer	0.56
A G Wickman	Burial of two outlaws	50.00
H E Stuart	Reg Births & Deaths in Lynden	6.00
	MARRIAGE CERTIFICATE FUND.	
F W Moses, Co Clerk	Recording Marriage Certificates	37.00
W K Sickles, Clk King Co.	do	2.00

----------oOo----------

Claim of Roland G Gamwell for 35.00 for Premium on bond of Court Stenographer, was endorsed "Refused" by the Board.

----------oOo----------

The November report of C C King, Supt Co Home, was approved by the Board.

----------oOo----------

The November report of O E Beebe, County Physician, was approved by the Board.

----------oOo----------

The Board made an order correcting the 1912 personal tax against Henry Slade, same being a double assessment.

----------oOo----------

On motion the Board adjourned to meet on Wednesday, December 9, 1914.

C B Logan
Chairman Board County Commissioners

Whatcom County commissioners' register showing $50 expense for "Burial of two outlaws"

GRAVE NO.	DECEASED NAME AND LAST KNOWN ADDRESS	SEX	CAUSE OF DEATH	BURIAL PERMIT NO.	DIED MO.	DAY	YR.	AGE YR.	DAY	MO.	INTERRED MO.	DAY	YR.
11	JOHNSON NELS	M	Apoplexy (MORTICIAN)	2207	5	24	09	72			6	23	09
12	CARLSON ALBERT	M	Tuberculosis (MORTICIAN)	3413	2	4	14	43			2	6	14
13	PETERSON PETER	M	Nephritis (MORTICIAN)	3446	3	30	14	70			3	31	14
14	FINNAN HUGH	F	Suicide (MORTICIAN)	3511	Found 6	29	14	59			7	1	14
15	UNKNOWN	M	Shot, Sedro Woolley Bank Robber (MORTICIAN)	3576	10	24	14	35			10	27	14
16	UNKNOWN	M	Shot, Sedro Woolley Bank Robber (MORTICIAN)	3577	10	24	14	35			10	27	14
17	DENNISH A.	M	Shot, Suicide (MORTICIAN)	3694	4	9	15	42			4	12	15
18	ANGELES GEORGE	M	Burned in lodging house (MORTICIAN)	3913	2	2	16	24			2	5	16
19	INFANT UNKNOWN MADEEN INFANT		Criminal negligence during confinement / Two Infants in grave 19 (MORTICIAN)	4148 4515	1 1	6	17 18				2 2	1 6	17 18
20	SIGURDSON M.	M	Syphilis (MORTICIAN)	4866	6	23	17	37			6	28	17

SEC. NO. F LOT NO. Potter's Field GRAVE NO. 11-20

Cemetery burial record from Bayview Cemetery in Bellingham, WA.

75

Current view of the entrance to Bayview Cemetery in Bellingham, WA where two of the four dead outlaws are buried.

The "Potters Field" at Bayview Cemetery in Bellingham, WA where two of the four dead outlaws are buried in unmarked graves.

5

False Leads & Returning to Life

A lso on October 27, the Bellingham Herald reported that Governor Lister of Washington State announced the state would pay a $500 reward for the apprehension of the remaining bank robber. The following day, $500 from the State for "apprehension, arrest, and conviction" was increased by another $500 by Skagit County for "the body – dead or alive".

While the search for the fifth bandit continued, a bit of comedy was experienced by posse members who were on early morning duty on October 28 at the railroad bridge in Ferndale. The headlight from Sheriff Wells' car that had been rigged to the bridge was still in place. Just after midnight, a hobo started to walk across the bridge. He was very loud and clumsy, and when he reached the point where the bandits had been killed, a posse member switched on the light. "He stared at the light a moment, then at the heavens, and finally started hunting around the track to see if he had stepped on some push button, and in that way, turned on the light. Seeing no button, he scratched his head, swore, and started off. One of the posse members on watch called for him to hold up his hands. The hobo lost no time in obeying his commend, getting on his tip-toes and hopping around like a Russian dancer," reported the Bellingham Herald on October 28, 1914.

Later in the morning on October 28, Sheriffs Thomas and Wells officially announced that they were abandoning the massive search for the last bandit, which left the region unguarded for the first time in ten days. On the same day, Deputy Charles Stevenson from Skagit County interviewed Mr. Leiver, one of the suspects, and decided to move the man to the Skagit County jail later in the day. He was later released when no evidence could be found to convict him of a crime.

On Monday, November 9, Sheriff Wells went to Seattle to follow a clue that the last of the Sedro-Woolley bank robbers may be in that area. The man was arrested in a pool room after having been followed for several days by Wells and Walter Thayer, manager of Burns Detective Agency in Seattle. Wells returned to Mount Vernon the afternoon of Wednesday, November 11 with the man who gave his name as Haig Kazansais, a Russian born Armenian. Kazansais was positively identified by Guddall in Mount Vernon as one of the men who had been loitering around his bank the week before the robbery. Despite the identification, no money or firearms were found, nor other evidence that could convict him of being part of the crime ring. He was later released.

Wells and Thayer were also given information about the location of the remaining stolen loot. Someone informed them that the $6,000 and an automatic revolver were buried in the woods north of Seattle, however they were never reported to have been found.

On November 12, 1914, the Mount Vernon Herald reported that Coroner Thompson of Whatcom County turned over the money from the robbers killed in Ferndale to the First National Bank in Sedro-Woolley. While he was aware of the law that said the treasurer would hold the money for six years before turning it over to the state school fund, Thompson determined that the law only applied when the money lawfully belonged to an individual. Because authorities were certain that this money was from the October 17 bank robbery, it was returned to the bank. On December 10, 1914, the Mount Vernon Herald further reported that Whatcom County commissioners took away Thompson's salary as punishment for turning the money over to the First National Bank. Thompson countered that what he did had been lawful and had the consent of the Whatcom County Auditor, but commissioners determined the money should have remained until it was claimed, per the written law. Thompson added that he was considering legal action for the return of his salary.

Following the bank robbery, photographs of the aftermath of the shootout, and of the dead bank robbers were compiled as glass lantern slides along with a script and presented in local theaters before feature films. Most of the photographs in this book are from those original glass lantern slides. The first showing of these images was in the Rex Theatre in December of 1914. When Sheriff Ed Wells' photo appeared on screen, the crowd broke out in applause. During this first showing, the lecturer paused at the image of the spotlight placed on the bridge in Ferndale, and three gunshots rang out from behind the screen for special effect. Startled, many audience members screamed and jumped from their seats.

On New Year's Day 1915, Sheriff Wells was honored by the First National Bank, and was presented a souvenir badge for his efforts following the robbery. The badge was sterling silver and engraved "Sheriff of Skagit County" on the front. The center of the badge was a $5 gold piece with an indentation from a bullet hitting the coin as one of the robbers was being fired upon. The back of the badge read "Presented to Sheriff Ed Wells by First National Bank, Sedro-Woolley, as a souvenir for splendid service in bandit chase, October 1914."

A letter was also presented to the sheriff, which read,

"Mr. Ed Wells
Sheriff of Skagit County
Mount Vernon, Wash.

Dear sir: On behalf of the bank, I am presenting you with a little token of remembrance of the chase and the two battles with the bandits at Hazelmere, B.C. and Ferndale, Washington in October, 1914. This coin was one of several, which were bent by bullets in these fights. We trust that you will find pleasure in wearing it. In this connection, I want to thank you for the splendid service you rendered, for we recognize that it was due to your good judgment, energy, and sticktoittiveness that this lawless band was finally wiped out. Trusting that all future work for you will be less hazardous and wishing you the most happy and prosperous New Year, I am

Yours very truly,
J. Guddall,
Cashier

Apologies for the quality of this image. Photo is of the commemorative badge presented to Sheriff Wells, which had been framed and was hanging in his son's house in 1996.

A photo of Sheriff Wells, framed and hanging next to the commemorative badge in his son's home during a 1996 interview.

1996 photo of the New Westminster, B.C. grave site of Clifford Adams, the Canadian immigration officer who was killed in Hazelmere, B.C. The inscription reads, "James Clifford Adams, 2nd Son of Mr. & Mrs. Geo. Adams. Shot while performing his duty as a Customs Officer. Oct. 22, 1914. Aged 25 years.

A letter received recently by the Sedro-Woolley Museum from the daughter of Deputy Fred Roessel, who is featured on the cover of this book.

I am an woman, born in 1909, crippled, but — my memories are still what I call "sharp". I have clear memories of when — 1914, I was 5 years old — Lennox my dad Fred Roessel — about 45 years coming home + telling my mother he had a job. The job was to go to the Ferndale bridge over the Nootsack River and intercept bank robbers. My mother was crying as she held my baby brother Glen.

She sed, "don't go and get killed, I cannot raise these four kids alone!!"

My Dad was a sheriff and duty called. Sheriff who was written about in the "True Detective magazine." (some where I have a copy of the story) Telephone was used then to spread the word

2/

I also remember Dad was given a $10⁰⁰ gold piece as his share of loot! Wish we had that now! But those were when a dollar was big money.

Good luck in reviving old History — If I can help in any way call me —

Maybelle R. Hotell

6

Epilogue

The story of the Great Sedro-Woolley Bank Robbery has now surpassed 100 years and remains firmly cemented in the lore of Sedro-Woolley history. For nearly 20 years, the Sedro-Woolley Museum has orchestrated a re-enactment of the robbery and resulting shootout as part of its annual Founders' Day celebration in September.

In all, the bulk of this extensive story spans a relatively brief period of just six days from the robbery until the death of the third and fourth outlaws. On foot, these men covered an impressive 85 miles from Sedro-Woolley, WA to Hazelmere, BC and back to Ferndale, WA. Even more impressive - or perhaps lucky - was the tracking by law enforcement officers, considering the rough and vast terrain between these towns with plenty of place to hide, primitive roads, and scarce police technology. The lawmen did benefit from a citizen's posse organized with haste that could rival today's social media communication, and watchful farmers and housewives along the way performed a service to the community that cannot be overstated.

In the end, just four of the five bandits earned the ultimate punishment as their "Wages of Sin". Very little is known about these four men who were believed to be Russians. Names were mentioned but were never made official, and the men received burials in unmarked graves. Buried with them was the story of their lives, their families, and explanation of the reason for the path they took in life.

Buried also were the opportunities for Melvin Wilson and Clifford Adams to live long, prosperous lives. Melvin was a bright-eyed teen whose life was cut short so needlessly. His family mourned for the innocence of youth being shattered in their once safe town. Clifford became one of so many lawmen taken out of this life during the call of duty. Even at such a young age, he showed great potential and earned high praise for his service and dedication.

Aside from the casualties, the citizens of northwest Washington and British Columbia were quite fortunate for the generally poor aim of this group of outlaws. With hundreds of shots fired between the original battle and the proceeding gunfights further north, the potential for dozens of lives to be lost was quite real.

Roughly $6,000 of the $11,649 in gold and silver taken from the First National Bank was ever found, leading to speculation as to the whereabouts of the remaining gold. Did the fifth bandit, who escaped the fate of his co-conspirators, make off with the money? Was Haig Kazansais fortunate enough to have stashed the loot before being arrested in Seattle, then return to it after being released? Or does it remain buried somewhere between British Columbia and Seattle near somebody's backyard 100 years later? Treasure hunters take note, the gold that is unaccounted for amounts to nearly $400,000 based on today's gold prices!

As mentioned earlier, one of the biggest lessons from this story for me, the author, wasn't in the story itself, but in the recording of it. While the big news of October 1914 in Sedro-Woolley could have been left to the newsmen and the authorities, some well intended citizen took the time to document nearly every step in this week-long unfolding drama. These stunning photographs captured the scenes and people involved with meticulous care and became a source of community pride in remembering the valor of citizens and officers in apprehending the dangerous gang. And they lived on in their fragile glass state for the next century as memories of the events the night of October 17th faded and generations passed.

Every day, history is being made all around us. Just as some folks did in 1914, our job is to document and record that history to be sure that it is preserved for future generations.

History's lessons are ours to remember.
When we lose sight of the lessons learned,
history repeats to remind us.

SOURCES

- "Bandit Battle Described by Detective." Bellingham Herald, Oct. 23, 1914

- "Bandit Hunt is Abandoned by Posses." Bellingham Herald, Oct. 28, 1914

- "Bandit Money is Cause of Trouble." Mount Vernon Herald, Dec. 10, 1914

- "Bandit Money may go into State School Fund." Bellingham Herald, Oct. 27, 1914

- "Bandit Suspect will be Held by Skagit County." Bellingham Herald, Oct. 27, 1914

- "Bank Presents Wells with Handsome Badge." Mount Vernon Herald, Jan. 7, 1915

- "Depict Story of Bank Robbery." Mount Vernon Herald, Dec. 17, 1914

- "Hold Alleged Bank Robber." Mount Vernon Herald, Feb. 25, 1915

- "Identity of Outlaws is made by Banker." Bellingham Herald, Oct. 24, 1914

- "May be the Other Bandit." Skagit County Times, Nov. 12, 1914

- "No Trace of Sedro-Woolley Outlaws is Found." Bellingham Herald, Oct. 19, 1914

- "Police Arrest Bohemian on Suspicion of Robbery." Bellingham Herald, Oct. 26, 1914

- "Posses on Trail of Fleeing Men." Mount Vernon Herald, Oct. 22, 1914

- "Returns Money to Robbed Bank." Mount Vernon Herald, Nov. 12, 1914

- "Robbers are Headed for Boundary Line." Bellingham Herald, Oct. 21, 1914

- "Robbers Identified by Seattle Police." Mount Vernon Herald, Nov. 5, 1914

- "Sedro-Woolley Outlaws Surrounded, and Pitched Battle Occurs at Border." Bellingham Herald, Oct. 22, 1914

- "The First National Bank Looted by Robbers last Saturday Evening, $11,649 Taken Away." Skagit County Times, Oct. 22, 1914

- "Two Bandits are Killed at Ferndale." Bellingham Herald, Oct. 24, 1914

- "Two Bandits Reported Surrounded by Posses." Bellingham Herald, Oct. 20, 1914

- "Two More Bandits Killed." Skagit County Times, Oct. 29, 1914

- "Wells Arrests Alleged Bandit." Mount Vernon Herald, Nov. 12, 1914

- Narration accompanying glass lantern slides. Date of origin and author unknown.

- Personal interview with Ethel Lemley, Daughter of John Guddall, March 8, 1995